The 1002nd Night

W9-CZU-932

Princeton Series of Contemporary Poets
For other books in the series, see page 74

The 1002nd Night

Debora Greger

PRINCETON UNIVERSITY PRESS

Copyright © 1990 by Princeton University Press
Published by Princeton University Press, 41 William Street,
Princeton, New Jersey 08540
In the United Kingdom: Princeton University Press, Oxford

All Rights Reserved

Library of Congress Cataloging-in-Publication Data
Greger, Debora, 1949-
The 1002nd night / Debora Greger.
p.   cm. — (Princeton series of contemporary poets)
ISBN 0-691-06863-1 (alk. paper) — ISBN 0-691-01492-2 (alk. paper)
I. Title. II. Title: 1002nd night. III. Series.
PS3557.R42T47   1990
811'.54—dc20   90-8270

Publication of this book has been aided by a grant from the
Lacy Lockert Fund of Princeton University Press

This book has been composed in Linotron Baskerville

Princeton University Press books are printed on acid-free
paper, and meet the guidelines for permanence and durability of
the Committee on Production Guidelines for Book Longevity
of the Council on Library Resources

Printed in the United States of America by Princeton
University Press, Princeton, New Jersey
       10 9 8 7 6 5 4 3 2 1
(Pbk.) 10 9 8 7 6 5 4 3 2 1

PS
3557
R42
T47
1990

3 3001 00812 2805

ACKNOWLEDGMENTS

Agni: "The New World," "Recent Events: The Fossil Record"

The Cambridge Review: "All Saints' Passage," "A Brief History of Blasphemy, for the Feast of the Assumption," "To a Mockingbird"

Denver Quarterly: "Action," "The Family Rilke," "The Opera Companion," "St. Jerome in an Italian Landscape," "The Report of the Corrosion Committee"

First Things: "A Reader's Guide to English Furniture: The Eighteenth Century"

The Gettysburg Review: "St. Jerome on the Virgin's Profession"

The New Republic: "Newton Wonders"

The New Yorker: "The Afterlife," "In the Elephant Folio," "Snow White and Rose Red"

Parnassus: "The Diamond of Devotion"

Poetry: "Narcissus," "The 1002nd Night," "The Rome of Keats," "Sleeping Beauty"

The Southwest Review: "A Guide to the Gods," "The Man Who Writes Dialogue for a Living," "The Temperate House," "On the Margins"

The William and Mary Review: "Don Giovanni in Florida," "Foolscap"

The Yale Review: "The English Tongue," "Ever After," "The Married State," "The Penguin Jane Austen," "Preface to the Collected Works"

Special thanks to the John Simon Guggenheim Memorial Foundation and the National Endowment for the Arts

for my father and mother

By the same author

Movable Islands
And

Now she had given directions to her young sister, saying to her, When I have gone to the King, I will send to request thee to come; and when thou comest to me, and seest a convenient time, do thou say to me, O my sister, relate to me some strange story to beguile our waking hour.

—*The Thousand Nights and One Night,* translated by Edward William Lane

She and her fictions soon were one.

—*"The Thousand and Second Night,"* by James Merrill

Contents

Preface to the Collected Works   3
The 1002nd Night   4
The Opera Companion   6
The Married State   11
On the Margins   13
Action   16
The Man Who Writes Dialogue for a Living   18
To a Mockingbird   20
The Rome of Keats   22
La Serenissima   23
St. Jerome in an Italian Landscape   27
St. Jerome on the Virgin's Profession   28
The Family Rilke   30
Sleeping Beauty   32
Recent Events: The Fossil Record   34
A Reader's Guide to English Furniture: The
    Eighteenth Century   35
The Penguin Jane Austen   37
The Little Mermaid Later   38
The Temperate House   41
Narcissus   42
The English Tongue   43
An English Suite   44
A Guide to the Gods   48
The Afterlife   50
A Brief History of Blasphemy, for the Feast
    of the Assumption   55
In the Elephant Folio   57
Foolscap   58
Snow White and Rose Red   59
The Report of the Corrosion Committee   61
The Diamond of Devotion   63
Ever After   71

The 1002nd Night

Preface to the Collected Works

Against the oceans' prose
overrunning seven-tenths of the planet,
against further fractions buried
by the plodding advance of ice caps,
glaciers' extended plots,
let these lines be shored
as the eel fisher would a platform
of reeds on a gravel bed, dwelling
where no invader would bother
but the odd missionary wading ashore,
sick on a surfeit of loaves and fishes,
plumping for the greater good
of a little slaughter, the conversion
into feed of winged flocks—
consider not just sins of commission
but omission as well, the shifting grounds
of argument for exclusion that,
bog dwelt upon too long, swallows the surveyor
preaching grand schemes of reclamation
to the unconverted on their higher perches.
Reader, recall the girl who,
by treading on the bread she'd been sent for,
saved herself from the downward tug of swamp
if not the hug of her mother's wrath.
Make good an escape here. On stoutest sea legs
flounder away from the punt the eelman poles
through weed-infested watermeadows
in a passage only he can divine.
Under his fen-fevered eye,
his catch squirms in slimed cursive
as he weighs not one squiggle against another
but lumps the smelly lot for what it's worth:
a roast on the table, a Sunday off.
Him in his eel-dark suit praising fish
of good size and plentiful enough
to walk the narrows on, spearing and netting
as he goes. Thanks given for no traps poached.

The 1002nd Night

Like any husband lying
beside a long-held wife, mine stretches,
ear to pillow's beached shell,
the heart's dim chambers awash with waves.

In the women's quarters a door shudders
on the days I lay landlocked
like a sailor turned weaver,
a knot for each night

the heavens tattered overhead
while, robed as lioness, given leash
to toy with prey, I told tales
as much to a lizard on the window grille

as to a husband holding my life in his palm.
Heart a lazuli pebble,
a lapis pulse under lunar skin,
the lizard fed me scant regard,

caught by the oil lamp's flickering tongue.
Knotted in our makeshift firmament,
Draco and Virgo fixedly drifting
neither into conjunction nor apart—

I went on, betraying nothing,
faithful at least to the story's letter,
and couldn't say that fear nursed grudge
those small hours. A near-human cry

slit the desert shadow, peahen baiting cock,
then deeper voices fishtailed from hearing,
the cloths men had spread to collect the dew
waiting to be wrung of their jewels.

I watched a dune shift grain by grain
the hourglass's heavy sleep
as dawn rain slipped unremarked
into a tale of northern kingdoms,

stealing through an everyday forest,
piercing the canopy of needles
to whip the cottonwoods' quivering leaves
into fistfuls of foreign coins

flung at a dancer walking from work
through the understory. First light hardens
where it strikes the cleaned bones
of the only two stories,

a man goes on a journey, a stranger
rides into town—bones of the one told twice,
once from his view, once mine.
From ribbed clouds a moon tugs the far seas

farther away, ivory gates flooding wide
at a breath. A salt caravan sifts
a fresh-swept page of sand: *A husband lies*
beside a long-held wife,

her dim heart's chambers awash with waves.

COSÌ FAN TUTTE

Qual prova avete voi, che ognor costanti
Vi sien le vostre amanti?

In dresses stiffly ribboned as Victorian houses,
two women at the edge of a quarrel
sublimely trill it into a small concerto.

At the blonde's muscled throat,
a miniature pulses—her lover cavalier
against flames: passion's pitched battle,

its chill hearth. As though neither
can hear the other, they hurl their secrets
in sly modulations toward us, fourth wall

of their house—whether to change lovers
like dresses to match another dazzling
Neapolitan day. Painted, the bay's silk

ripples around islands anchored firmly
as love in a deep bed; the volcano smolders,
rouging the horizon. Powdered bosoms swell

over full lungs, the ache of harmony's thirds
baring an isolation never hinted,
pulsing under the score by a man who

in 1787 wrote to his father that,
of companions, death is the most faithful.

CALLAS

Ascolta!

Up through ranks of lowly marigolds
calla lilies push, budding divas
in understudy unswaddling ivory throats,
preening for dressing-room mirrors

in the starched ruffs of *Maria Stuarda*.
Lopped, they crowd a vase next to paints
for a face sunned by holidays spent
at a score's flyspecks until had by heart

amid arching scales and arpeggios.
Over the intercom a voice scrambles onstage,
ascending stairs of another story:
husband taken care of this nuptial night

by her own hand, the single petals
of Lucia's spotless sleeves bell open.
Her light fingers twine spotlit air
to a fakir's rope snaking upward

into the flies, high mad notes wobbling
up the sturdy stalk of a hothouse bloom
as she wilts. Fioriture
trained to take the knife in character,

the lilies didn't flinch from the florist
whose blade failed to retract.
They bowed, professional as the white dress
of the girl who faced soldiers, trading fire:

arias for sweets to fatten three voices
too big for her—a low range,
its drops veiled by the mirage
of reedy middle tones that flooded the hall

without quenching a top note's florescence.
On her dressing table, in with other spills,
pollen spends its overbright powder.

DON GIOVANNI IN FLORIDA

Le finestre son queste; ora cantiamo.

Wind's base aspirations flutter palmetto fans
in the face of a mute chorus, windows gaping
at pollen gilding suspended quarrels

and snatches of another music,
Italian for how many women a man's had.
A rake rattles the neighborhood gossip

of magnolia leaves, the entanglements
of Spanish moss draped in shawls
over bared arms of sweet-gum branches.

Che bella notte, the famous rakehell sings,
for hunting girls, strolling a graveyard.
Past the jaws of two plastered lions,

under a singer teetering from a second story,
women in flowered frocks dot a fraternity lawn,
mimicking the white crocus that depends

on chillier states to open,
plastic cups of flattened beer
leaning to toast conquest of anything:

a soprano's *No, non ti credo* brushed aside;
the *galantuomo*, good profligate,
making little deaths in the arms of desire

do for more gripping darkness,
his voice silkily lifting skirted curtains,
worming its way in.

BARNUM'S SWEDISH NIGHTINGALE

She claims I exhibited her as good
as next to Chang and Eng or General Tom Thumb,
but what grounds? Europe she'd taken by song,
but who'd taken note here? "A dancer?"
guessed the conductor of trains I asked.
So I made her yours, all but the voice,
and that, I loved her to say, borrowed from birds,
in her avian accent. What to exhibit?
Had she been half a set of Siamese twins
who harmonized, or bird-sized,
had feathers for that flaxen hair—
plumage like the warbler's I can report
sang with her till it fell dead at our feet—
herding her twittering flock
four thousand miles for ninety-three concerts
wouldn't have been enough campaign
for this old campaigner, nor I still
my own best advertisement. But, her mouth shut,
what marked her from you, my often vocal public?

I applaud the one of you who sold me her portrait
in oils, gilt-framed, fifty dollars,
knowing what I didn't till later:
the look of a lithograph varnished on tin
worth thirty-seven cents. This way
to my Great American Museum and Menagerie:
human statues, trained seals almost human.
This way to the Egress.

The Married State

*T*o the hawk drifting in vague rings
above Nevada, scouting for kill,

plight thermal air currents plaiting their columns
into ghost ruins of the temple

still supporting a fragment of frieze
where feet carved in relief trample the remains

laid out in stone of a wedding feast
that fire, more forgiving, would spit at

as at the virgins vowed once to its endless tending.
To tumbleweed, bind telephone pole,

guy-wired upright the lone prospect
on the wind-defiled plain. Their embrace

half thorn, half handful of splinters—
to the garden of Elsewhere their woods stand for,

to long-distance lines wordlessly murmurous
of that static hush descending

more before sleep's little deaths
than speech's, pair the highway motel,

where split seconds lodge their silence
between a past caught underwheel

as trucks haul through the night,
and the animal sadness coming after,

downshifting into futures tearing away.
To proposals unmet, couple the direct approach

down from switchbacks of bare hills
to hot air licking pavement wet,

roadbed's tease melting ahead
into glimmers of clear invitation,

mirage that dries itself in a flourish
as a single car nears.

To the arrow of light bulbs chasing each other,
on and off, up to the pilasters of Zeno's Casino

without shooting inside, pledge full houses
come again. To air-conditioned plush,

to plump rolls of complimentary coins
keen to shake loose each other

and be swallowed by swift machinery
of state, tender each face

of the soon-to-be-sundered couples,
the summarily tied, their promised,

their compromised hands to the handles
of machines responding heartlessly

with probability's ill-matched threesomes of fruit.

On the Margins

After the Low Countries, Reader,
turn back, turning out the small pocket
in the seam between larger powers,
a smuggler's pouch the shape of Andorra
counting on being passed over as always,
small potato at one with those rolled loose
from their ox-driven wagon and wedged
between boulders' ice-age guard
shouldering the one municipal road.
Overlook, as the brief entry does
from lofty vantage, a main valley
that highroad and one river thread—
how they contrive to needle shepherds
and brigands alike, long-frozen passages
halting even the most stir-crazed raider.
Its rulers rival each other for inaction,
stalemated bishop holding in check a prince
over country jointly held not worth dispute.
Sleep inbred in its snows, landlocked island
unreachable by air, railless,
its passes blocked for ages—still
the odd anthropologist makes his way
to the one hotel, where he stumbles
upon luggage abandoned by another of his kind
belaboring the lift to effect transhumance

up a floor, machine in medieval dialect
unburdening itself the while with groans
of a steep-pitched room letting slide
a year's thatch of snow. Six-fingered streams
swarm the one street while, higher,
snow's altar cloths stripped away,
peaked dustcovers prostrate
before a hunting lodge's mounted heads,
smugglers the mountains claimed in duty
lie revealed, well preserved as local saints
tucked between *anachronism* and *anomaly*,
sporting their cloth-of-gold.

IN THE HEAVEN OF SIDEKICKS

Esteemed members of the Academy,
leading men and ladies whose names balloon
from the tongues of talk-show hosts
into the starry firmament of fame
above the titles of movies beneath which we flicker
and are extinguished in smaller type,
extend your regard as your hand,
acting a storm, would stretch forth
to calm seas of dry ice,
toward us old reliables
where we lounge and swagger
safely out of camera range,
having lunged and staggered,
picked off in our prime.
Draw closer if I fail to reach you,
drawing closer your furs to upstage
the air conditioner acting up.
Unamplified, let me wax eloquent
as apples ruddy in rude boxes
on those who neither soften
nor go bad, the cowhands who rode herd
fattening for your prodigal return,
well versed at stepping out of the way
through lines of fire, catching stray bullets,
common colds, rare diseases,
and misfired bridal bouquets one-handed.
Relaxed as ventriloquists' retired dummies,
we grant audience in front of televisions
snapped to attention—"The Late Show" where,
in snippets between commercials
likely to feature you as well,
household words trading on your bankable names,
we ride again into no sunsets.

Action

RISING

*R*oots tied to wormed hollows
a spade cuts clean. On its sharp tongue
dirt's rich cake steams as if turned
from its pan to cool, crumbling at the edges—

but icing can slather over such ravage
with roses. Gowned and veiled
with flour, a baker sweats over petals
built into bloom, his forehead beaded,
his shop window, too. Not standing
on ceremony, he roots a marzipan couple
in the virginal snow of the cake's top tier—
so they list a little, sugar creme
frosting their shoes, still they look
nowhere, not even to each other,
but ahead, needing no rehearsal
to face priest, judge, ship's captain,
or camera. Beyond the window's heaped altars,

black-frozen leaves crunch under the scrubbed
sensible shoes of a nurse skirting the barrows,
the burrows of roadwork, the crew's grimy glance
whistling suggestions at her clean whites.
In a raveling sweater, light-colored once
when someone knit it for him, a man lowers
into a ditch until he's just shovel's edge
and dirt flung to the crest of a mound,
its rising sliding into dénouement.

FALLING

The kiss of one ball knocking another
down billiards' ripe field, that's how calculated
should be the join of the tight-compassed circles
he skates—but a figure eight stumbles,
lopsided infinity fallen from grace.

Up from the cold cushion smacked in the middle
of daydream, he pushes off, stroking half an eight:
three's two cups for the threesome
that's blade, ice, and onshore coach
cradling laced coffee in a Thermos cup.

Its steam cuts a small window's trace
in the wall of stony cold the skater skirts.
He could be on its other side, running
a moistened finger round the rim
of a glass till wine and crystal screamed

their joint rounded note as if
outlining a breast—but he sights
three feet ahead at another melting,
old friction scrawled on penmanship's desk.
Up from the sheaf of shore,

a red cup's swash initials a fresh page
as it waves him on, champion at the going
and going over of rings and zeros,
the white ink of his coach's voice spilling,
demanding just that he stay

on the tracings—O to stay on.

The Man Who Writes Dialogue for a Living

*a*scends an on-ramp looped as calculatedly
as the *C* leading to "Come on in,"
an opening line he's summoning up,

like a parking-lot valet, for a champion surfer
to sputter away, or some corporate head,
raving through lines broad as lanes,

one interchange engineered after another
by this stout Cortez commuting
from the Pacific's poolside,

talking in air-conditioned intimacy
to a tape recorder. To his reclusive canyon's foot,
maid, nanny, gardener, and chauffeur bend,

descending from a bus for the hike
to their stations, speaking among themselves
the Spanish for minor characters

with their own plots to thin after hours:
cilantro's bitterness cultivated for seasoning,
crowded by *yerba buena*'s migrant family

whose extras carpet the hills
with spearmint's expired green cards
under the hoofs of a horse urged on

by his daughter, more eloquent
with her knee and heel than mouth.
It's another gorgeous day on the soundstage,

an unnamed planet swimming a black-hung sky.
Models of a peak in Darien, inverted,
commissary cups slop their silence

on the clamorous oceans of margin
licking the flotsam of speech, the jetsam
of first rewrite, and second, blowtorches rushing

the salvage yard of mild surmise.

To a Mockingbird

*J*ust another Mozart in black and white,
tailfeathers fanned in arpeggio,
you mock the clavier with your drab livery
and lilting ornaments; mock the prodigy

called upon by kings to improvise,
handkerchief hiding the keys,
who so improves upon his masters
he masters them; mock with your snappy,

sappy bows the roadhouse king of song
reprising the tune that bought his title.
King partial to more cultivated lands
but taking as your due wild smilax,

nightshade, prickly pear, and fig,
you grant no audience requests for favorites
but move from phoebe to flicker, belted kingfisher,
through the broken song of the red-eyed vireo,

praising yourself in other voices
because all praise hollows in double time.
Caught and sold, you mock from your cage
the clock's unleashed alarums,

spring the hours from their ordained order,
your own time measured in moonlight
kept constant by streetlamps' quavers.
Just another Mozart in borrowed summerhouse,

neither wife nor wine urges your overture
onto paper, clean sheets of it
past waiting up for half or quarter rests.
If someone flutters out of winter's reach

into some museum, his sodden shoes
on marble will wring sobs
from the controlled air, the catch
of his breath fog the glass

that seals an urn hermetically,
its cracked lovers repaired
to the English glade the radiators sing of,
sealing each hiss with a moan.

Gone from the long-faced windows
the powdered pompadours of chestnut bloom,
the jaunty cockades of mimosa
long since limped from the field.

The air you teased alive with absences
fills now and again with the minor thirds
of mourning doves' fogbound notes,
that beauty's mockery, mockery truth

not enough to feed on these midwinter months
you're silent save for the odd harsh *chuck*,
no match against the flageolets
of cardinals' lusty *whip whip whip*.

The Rome of Keats

A slash of rain dully pierces the Tiber
as it did the too-heavy coat
of his companion, the one with the name

of an English river, who fled sickroom
for the dank, fresh eternal city.
The rain inscribes nothing,

sliding the Spanish Steps into hazard
where tubercular linens slumped in a pyre.
At two removes under its locket of glass,

a fair lock of hair curls on itself
like a barber-surgeon's leeches
bone-dry in their jar. A brittle cough

of wind rattles the museum,
brutal as paper with age: *half in love*
with easeful death. Rain scans equably

the man hawking boxes of body parts
stamped in tin, waiting to be tacked
to shrines and healed by prayer;

and streaks the overstressed make-up
of women staggered, gaudy off-rhymes,
against the train station,

lyrically accenting nothing not for sale.
Glazed with its fine, cheap film,
at the Protestant Cemetery we pay

the keeper as if it were something to own,
the stone carved with the name unwritten by water.

La Serenissima

Most serene, most squandered republic,
city of street Madonnas,
of church-porch statues holding heavenly court,

after centuries of vigilant sleep through afternoons
whose drawn shades stitched and tacked
salt breezes into sails for your fleet,

its plunder of watered silks stretched past you,
wakeful undreamed-of nights attended by women
with favors for sale. Some came cheaply

as the Virgin's vigil lights,
whose avid tongues licked at church wall and door
until the blue Lady of the Evening

and her ladies-in-waiting burned in masquerade,
Inquisitors round an impassioned stake.

2

A swart glassblower mouthed the O of expulsion
smoothly as an angel at your water gate
sweating under his mask as he handed you down

to your gondola. So, city of masques, you swayed forth.
A moon lopsided with luster traced the wake
your boat spun out all night,

encrusting with light's lifted jewels
the sticky web of canals,
the gondolier to refuse your husband,

should he be home, where you surfaced
and in whose arms, or drown at the hands
of the brotherhood of gondoliers.

3

Your islands' sodden fagots lashed in nets
of sloshed light, a *cavaliere servente* laced you
into another evening's fallen chandelier of gown,

mindful of make-up smeared down your breasts,
that you'd dance attendance yourself
upon the one surface untouched,

the sky dismantling fireworks' embroidery.
After the fired blooms of artifice
had been unpicked, he'd see you rowed to the Lido

to bathe your eyes in flames of a diluted dawn:
shades of the dew minted green
for your bath and dashed with musk and myrrh,

of the red-gold dyes tinting your hair
the gilt of the basilica's pate
turned brazen at sunrise as a husband just home.

4

Daughter of salt farmers, wife of the sea,
good name in mud, your cavalier dipping veal in milk
to cleanse your face, in the home of the mirror

you peeled off a beauty patch—a *sfrontata*
from a powdered nose, signaling forwardness,
or a *passionata* that had winked beside a kohl-rimmed eye,

or, kissing the corner of your painted mouth,
an *assassina* still at work, as saucy as the spots
decorating your lagoon: isle of disease

and of the dead, of lace-making orphans,
the female mad, the male insane.

5

So many crumbs for the Piazza's spoiled pigeons,
for the painter of your portrait,
working in model first, carving a cheese

step by step to bridge the ratty water
of worktable, reaching for the dried bread
of *campo* and *scuola*, sliced

in perspective's fashionable wedge.
Strung up between crumbling *palazzi*,
your wax and cotton likeness allowed him the liberty

of arranging the frills for your shadow's fall.
At Carnival the bodies of the hanged
twirled above you, masked, just so.

6

City of mirrors, city of spies,
when the maker who sold you quicksilvered wares
sold their secret to courts abroad,

you wasted no reflection, had him hunted,
dragged home, held in a cell whose floor
seeped water too dark to catch the rats

hanging like ermine on the sleeves
of titled worthies who once mocked
such rabid servants of the sumptuary laws.

7

City of unsigned denunciations
flooding the Doge's palace with the foul waters
of leisure: diamond-engraved city,

leaf-gilded, fired, frosted vessel
of fluid grace, vase in a galleon's shape,
urn holding ashes, bone's reliquary:

sinking ghost gliding the green-sequined Grand Canal
past the pocked faces of palaces
flinching in waterstained mirrors

where your boat slashes its ornamental, dissolute blade:
city most loyal to her own reflection.

St. Jerome in an Italian Landscape

*W*ind warm as breath, rough
    as a lion's grateful tongue, perfumed
like women masking their muskiness:
    to the wild poppies it ministers,
brushing against their skirts,
    grazing the painted mouths
they purse, upturned. They'd deny it
    nothing, swayed by its pitch—
four years in the desert he burned

and with him Rome, again, its maidens
    dancing flames around him
over catacombs where he longed to lie
    in the rictus of prayer instead.
Nights coupled days; scorpions danced
    attendance on his every blink
and he blessed their little whips
    that their cloister take him in.
No flagellant is the charcoal maker

belaboring his burden of willow switches
    toward a vision: a column of smoke
promising hot food, and more come market day.
    Nor the man upon the scaffolding
in the valley church who,
    after he limned a lion
preying on nothing more meaty
    than fellow symbols of faith,
broke bread and rubbed its bulk

of tempted flesh away.

St. Jerome on the Virgin's Profession

*F*rom sparrow to soldiers laid out
on their respective fields,
all things can your Father raise up

but a virgin fallen
to the down pillows of luxury
such as you're accustomed to.

Let your gowns dye parchment purple,
gold melt to leaf for lettering,
jewels flower upon manuscripts—next

by the false waters of loneliness
you'll lie, skirts hiked up,
veiling your face to any man passing by.

Dodge the roomy litters of widows,
and their troops of eunuchs,
neighborhoods where lust sprawls

next door to wantonness and,
after immoderate suppers, desire
quenched by desire, the women

retire to dream of the apostles.
Even in your own house you're not safe—
soft arms locked Samson up;

from his housetop King David's gaze
fell on Bathsheba, naked. Look
not too often on what you have

spurned but let sleep take you
on the sly, the sacred page
cushion your head. With your legs,

make musical the night
like the single grasshopper;
before she was driven from its garden,

there woman knew no shame
until she put on garments. Let the spring
be sealed, the fountain stilled,

wedlock be praised for giving birth to virgins.

The Family Rilke

*B*luing and salt, the bay's eye brimmed,
reflected, sloshed in a cup on the terrace
he had to himself that early
as he stripped off the striped top
of his bathing suit. In a wallow of solitude,
the bay blinked at nothing—not trunks
dropped on a rock. Not the blotch
that was a nude in the water, his teeth beginning
to chatter at maids clouding the terrace
with tablecloths and talk, keeping him submerged.

This was the easy part, alone, rich
with audience, blue-gray packets of letters
stroking north to wife and daughter,
to court a patroness with discourse
on a swim's esthetics. The ascetic's dinner
of fruit and milk stood pushed aside
into still life, the sensual scratch
of pen against paper frothing a bluer wake.

And now the famous families we'd paid to see
made spangled entrance: The Tumbling Thises,
The Flying Thats—up near the tent's top,
pendulums cut from grandfather clocks,
they fling themselves into each other's
split-second-timed arms. Down in the ring,
a human pyramid rises from sawdust,
inverted triumph over the gravity
of taking a fall. How they depend on—
even *from*—each other, taking the air
with ease not so much inherited
as passed hand to hand: against sweat's slippage,
trade secrets of rosin and talc.
Against fallings-out, discipline that dazzles
by its thousand hours sewing down sequins
in separate trailers under different last names.

And here is my Switzerland, white-draped table
with Sir at his end, Madame at the other,
and I, apron starched into wings,
holding between them, dishing courses
like weather onto a country whose relief
is the rounds of china, candle, and glass.
The whites of cream soup, potato, meringue—
fallen farther than I in station,
snowflakes paste themselves at long windows
to look on as they melt from the outside in.

Another Switzerland is spread south,
where high in a borrowed castle my father lies.
Whitened by the snow to snow,
among trees fleshed out to plaster statues,
he cools as my mother's work did
to my touch. I've learned he loved
good linens almost more than the meals
laid for him in the houses of titled women.
These blue-gray letters were his eyes.

Sleeping Beauty

*B*elieved extinct these last seventy million years
but, snapping at the hand of the captain
who flopped it onto the deck of his trawler;

buried under the small sharks and spiny dogfish
that plumped and jeered the day's catch
with toothy, worthless grins,

it lay, living fossil fading from mauvy blue
to dirty, steely gray. Yet to be portaged
to a taxi on the dock and driver persuaded

the creature hadn't begun to reek,
though an equatorial December sun rained down
on overworked iceman and taxidermist alike;

not yet swaddled in formalin,
no shroud fashioned of old news;
nor laid in state for twenty thousand to view—

a bony lungfish caught by a kiss,
I was hauled in from sleep's unfathoming depths
to another life, where the scales worked in gold

on my farthingale marked me as other
than his upright subjects walking on their fins,
those too lowly to afford equipage or mount.

My eyes adapted to lowest light
over that century he claimed I had slept,
I favored the ultramarine hours

when the sheer weight of fine mist
submerged the new artfully natural grounds.
Trees stiffened to coral, palace sinking

to seafloor in so grave a progress
no crystal cracked, dark of the new moon
deepening the grotto to an underwater cave

where, cooler than surrounding ocean,
rainfall seeped, nothing out of place
but a handline the current suspended

obliquely down the water column
from a night-fisherman's pirogue
and, sodden handkerchief lost overboard,

a reward poster, its letters streaming,
proposing, *Look carefully at this fish.*
It may bring you good fortune.

Recent Events: The Fossil Record

*T*hrough the sedimentary museum
all that still moves is dust and a woman
dusting drawer upon drawer of stony specimens.

To each impressed foot and petrified tooth
her gloved hand fits a theory
only to discount it, expounding another

for why two bodies no longer join but rift.
A Paleozoic leaf recording its fall
in a carbon smear, butterfly wing pulled

from the Miocene, and already the New Life Era
exhibits stuffed quadrupeds, cabinets
standing firm on fanciful claws,

silk-stockinged bipedal scholars cataloguing faults.
Over their samples of bedding planes
she lays the dreamy methodical drift

of continents sundering, savage
in their extended courtesy, two centimeters a year.
Over this, over acid remarks recorded in passing

by a sea overriding a mountain's breakers
fading from seventeenth-century notes,
model dinosaurs bare vicious little plastic yawns.

A Reader's Guide to English Furniture: The Eighteenth Century

*F*orget the romance purveyed of window seats,
knocked as they be by the winds
that skim drowned lawns of all
but fleets of scavenger gulls.

Summer, a dandy assures us
from his portrait next to horse and hounds,
grooms the bay just out of sight.
Marquis, field marshal, bishop,

mistress of the king, two indolent wits—
for his guests the catch,
rough justice in the scales of the fish that,
baked whole and portaged from kitchen depths

up floors, down corridors, reaches the table
likelike as a still-wet still life and as cold.
Unsnagged from its dumb throat,
the rictus of a laugh lasts

to toast the next course, the hunt's game,
those who afford such spreads
come to afford the attendant gout as well.
And to order footstooled gout chairs fashioned,

carcasses of native oak veneered
with dusky woods of empire,
shellac made of parasite secretions
shipped from India to finish them.

And, damp evenings, to order the chair be drawn
to the fireplace, *Crusoe* laid ready,
fire built to a lush and private isle
balmy, as the footman Friday knows,

as long as there's wealth to be burnt
and someone, through much practice
master of the flint striker
but knowing his station, to stoop

and, in his best time of two minutes,
manage to light it for you.

The Penguin Jane Austen

With a single indecorous groan
a glacier calves an iceberg the size
of a cathedral into the christening sea.
Along the icefoot, ritual courtship

flurries the frigid air into squawks
and plumage, the shuffled chase
that observers, stomping their feet for warmth,
call dance. And after?

After a belle's dance card filled twice over
and a wallflower wilted with watching
territory staked step by measured step,
and the pecking order of kisses?

After the final bow,
after swallow-tailed males swooped
over the shimmer, the shiver
of jewel- and sweat-scaled females?

Up from the bed of lost feathers,
the mating for life. Under a sky
literate with *M*'s, littered
with scavengers' winged *W*'s,

two months stand still on the ice for him,
egg cradled on his melting feet.
For her the miles to retreating sea
to feed, then the longer walk back.

O cotillions and calling cards,
clergy waddling in wedding vestments,
marriage of property to title, awaiting issue,
how roughly do you compare?

The Little Mermaid Later

*R*ambling Rose, you named me,
    beached before your throne,
mute as the fish that had swum away when I,

    no longer its kind, my tail split
into feet I'd traded my tongue for,
    had floundered onto my land legs

and was found blubbering by a fisherman
    who swabbed from my face the other salt water
those in the upper world call tears.

    Sea Rose, you called me,
though Seaweed holding fast its rock inshore,
    laid bare by low tide to dry a little

toward death, would have come closer,
    the way I'd fixed upon Your Lordship
nights I'd surfaced under dark's cover

    in the wake of the royal barge,
sculling on my back, just another smaller vessel
    lit fitfully by such displays of temperament

as you afforded, stars fused of salts and powders
    booming open over us, gaudy as a greedy bed
of anemones swallowed by their own reflections.

    Big fish who couldn't swim,
you none too often lowered your blue-blooded body
    to the small pond of a crested tub.

Shrimp who turned pink in water
    brought nearly to boil, you decreed the wind
of your favor set to shift a few degrees,

too broad a sweep of your ringed and dripping hand
toward nobles who bordered on treason
     risking a slip by the barber-surgeon's blade

along your slathered throat. Freshly manicured,
     your hand you plotted giving in marriage
to one landed princess, or another,

          darting among their miniatures, goldfish round its bowl
chasing gold-leafed hair, a pair of lapis eyes.
     Ladies of the court wove the wedding tapestry,

first a body of water dyed with woad and black currant.
     Then a Neptune ruled streams and fountains,
salt waters and fresh sent over land he desired

          to possess or punish. Knot by knot,
mille fleurs were forced into bloom along the warp,
     the field they flowered raveling from shore.

A rocky outcrop fell, taking the folds of a gown.
     A hand stiffened, tilting a mirror
not to the veiled moon waiting a face

          but toward you, or me, bearing no likeness.
Cow, you would call me,
     had I stayed in your upper world,

winged fish racketing from hard branches
     under water swollen into whales of cloud
as my body thickened with age,

          and you'd have been half right.
Cousin to the elephant many times removed,
     to sailors half the world away

from wives dreaming them drowned,
    I'm siren serenading shipwrecks
until not a dry eye's left aboard.

    Sea cow who salutes a queen worth her weight
in water hyacinth, so buoyant
      back in my element you could lift me still,

I wave the five finger bones of a flipper
    at the males keeping court. Belly to belly,
as missionaries preach to remotest islanders

    is proper, we distract extinction
at the hands of your kind with what you called
    the little death. One of the young,

yet to learn better, gives the glass face
    of a diver's helmet what he will swear
to his party ashore—having advised the harbor

    be dredged, whatever scrapes loose
profiting study—could only be described,
    bristling in the depraved light, as a kiss.

The Temperate House

To be wanted so much—dug up live,
coddled across oceans, winched off ship,
and walled up. In the house built
around their tonnage, these trophies

of taxonomy want for nothing.
As quarantined as mistresses behind fans
painted with envy's green vistas,
their place is not here, queening

over the man who sweeps the gravel
of human detritus. Decaying in echoes
of far-off tattoos, rain drums the glass roof
of a country, not theirs,

where the tallest palm strains
toward a blazing, absent arch of sky.
Rafters and thatch, harpoon, blowpipe,
arrow shaft, oil and food—

they'll be none of those now.
Long names crowding tags, in quarters
cramped as deposed royalty camped in,
waiting for jewelry to be broken up and sold,

their peasant bearing spares them
neither the exile that is love stunted
nor the one hollowed from fear.
Steam's arabesques of abandon

go limp against the glass. In the algal pool,
I'm reflected green—the frequency unabsorbed
by all the leaves but given back,
least of what transpires, the only one seen.

Narcissus

Sloshed to their slender throats
in deep buckets, the forced narcissi bud,
the fluted taxi-yellow of their klaxons
flagging traffic to standstill.

Who has eyes for new potatoes
or the boy swooping them, stream-smooth stones,
into his full-grown hands? Between customers,
he preens in a pocket mirror

only to be damped by his father,
a river god misting bouquets of broccoli,
radish corsages and parsley boutonnieres.
Wielding a knife whose appetite

has whetted the blade to a slice of itself,
the boy shaves a cauliflower.
Flesh of firm unblemished apples,
sleek muscled body of water—

some think to court him over cucumbers and tomatoes,
to hang in echo on the little he mutters
to hurry them out of his shadow,
a crate of trimmings balanced on his ripe shoulder:

the limp, the bruised and gone-to-mold
destined to grace an altar roughed of empty boxes,
beauty exacting tribute where it may,
left to exalt itself in rank decline.

A brace of daffodils quivering in his back pocket,
he hoses the sidewalk's dry bed
free of carrot stub and lost cabbage leaf,
rude toy ferry the gutter swirls on its way.

The English Tongue

*A*ligned across a snowy Styrofoam tray,
six frozen New Zealand lamb tongues
offer themselves from the well-stocked altars

of the meat aisle, shoppers flanked
by red muscle the way clergy are outnumbered
at evensong by cheeky choristers. There,

fresh from bells' lashing, boy sopranos
arch their soft palates like the chapel ceiling.
Its miles of ribbed vaulting spread lacy fans

weighing tons, buttressed by the organ's brassy rumble.
A clerestory of upper-class vowels soars,
undoing sacrament, making flesh into words

for nothing more concrete than the stalwart flames
painted above the heads of apostles
about to plunge through glossolalia's cloud

to the spit of land that is the mother tongue.
A speech thick with lust for definition,
words for the licking of parts

of another's body to make love or commerce,
blackens with centuries like the shriveled trowel
of saint's tongue in its jewel-scabbed reliquary.

An English Suite

ALL SAINTS' PASSAGE

*T*o recut the border between unilluminated and unlit,
hard by a wall sandblasted from the Dark Ages,
the tempered sunlight sliced a wafer-thin walk

swallowed by the winter dusk. Out of a window
escaped from a window tax long dead,
facing the blind consecrated wall,

a school-leaver by rote removed the tidy jettison
of liqueur-filled seashells, the parade ground
of bonbons and decorated clusters

staggered in rows with soft-centered mounds,
the truffles laid in formation tight as tombstones,
and then undid her milky apron, her creamy cap.

Her cocoa-drab uniform ordered rank shadows
into darkness richly bittersweet where,
under ultraviolet light, the paper lace left out

crystallized to snow that fell no farther
onto the future-perfect declension of empire
than past three revolutions in confectionery

nor melted over pieces of eight that,
bitten, would give more than gold.
In lopsided halo they laid the name

of some likeness too dim to discern
at the base of a foil-wrinkled globe
dwarfed by a chocolate-cast pocket watch.

Lard and vinegar seasoned the raw air
at the day's last frying, fish and chips
warming a page of old news

even as they cooled and stiffened to the touch.

NEWTON WONDERS

*B*igger than two-fisted hearts,
apples knock their bright heads together
in display, greener than envy,

than vestments of hope, or Venus, named for love.
Blushing, they hold firm a law
over bodies in motion: that a body rests

or moves forever in a straight line
unless acted upon. Around the corner
of Adam and Eve Street, the single block

of Paradise issues with no outlet;
across town no Newton Wonders drop, fresh
as fallen angels at the feet of his statue.

There in the unrefracted Protestant light
of his college chapel, he suffers
neither the slights of incurious stares

nor the rain of dust rinsing his marbled curls
darker, younger than the hour after 1665—
merciless as the disturbance he has yet to prove

wafts its sound around obstacles,
or waves of light flushing the region of shade,
the Great Plague will fell a hundred thousand.

Schools emptied, an average scholar sent home
roughs his thinking outside: codling-moth larva
feeding at the apple's heart, on the first law

the second hosts, the one about force.

THE NEW WORLD

*R*owboats bailing equatorial waters,
armor beading and greening in the wet draw
that warps and shrinks a tall ship

like sucked candy: here on the sill
in a jar of raw honey, past crystal spars,
hulls of two bees spend days sinking

through the sweet stickiness,
a little heavier than rain
pocking a sea crossed with sun's last promise

of disease only gold can cure.
The honey floats thicker than water
where the crew's belts and shoes boiled,

seasoned with herbs, to be eaten
that the clotted throat of the hourglass might open,
the fog of indistinguishable knots part

and signs of land stretch into view—
no more motes in the eye nor a flock
of songbirds, too many to be strayed or lost,

but the mouth of the Orinoco, Ralegh's man asleep
under a ragged flag and, lying by him
in place of a secret wife, thirteen gold bars

for the taking. Armor rusted, clothes rotten,
food gone or gone bad: bearing the Old World
from its swamped boat, to steal

toward him so that his sleep stay unfathoming,
his mouthful of sand making dream-barter
that if there be lives more honeyed,

there be, at the hands of a royal executioner,
death closer to home as well.

A Guide to the Gods

*T*ier by tier we scale the Theatre Olympus
up to its cheapest seats to sit on our raincoats,
overlooking the circles' minor constellations

of paste, the boxes' major ones of gems,
and the starry eye of it all: actors
flailing like songbirds in a dustbath,

though you need the rental opera glasses
to tell blue tit from lesser spotted woodpecker.
High winds scouring our upper atmosphere,

their stage whispers shrink them further
to dolls perched on dollhouse furniture,
delivering secrets meant to carry to us

in lines Mnemosyne, our mother,
mouths from memory. Ranked beside her,
we daughters are gifted or cursed

by her forgetting nothing,
as she'll remind us at home:
how Thalia's darting laugh underscored all

the wrong moments abounding this evening;
Terpsichore's toe shoes clumping
in her mid-act getaway; Polyhymnia's letting slip

a fistful of ungraded essays
over the gallery's edge in rhetorical blizzard—
so many air-dropped leaflets aimed to take by surprise

classes unable to afford my luxuriously musing
upon a coup's bloodless rehearsal at intermission
by a black-clothed crew burlesquing revolt.

Her students' prose falls short,
catching off guard the sables and top hats
at ease beneath us—

to daydream history is not to hear
Mother's "Clio, come! It's over."
Up here, where the ceiling's peeling cherubs

drop crumbs of ambrosial plaster
in our laps, we're just like other gods
at work, sitting on our hands, bemused,

waiting to see how it comes out below,
breathing in the rarefied foul air
that beggars pride.

The Afterlife   *in memory of Howard Moss*

THE LIGHT DRESS

> But now a year has passed and we can think of it calmly;
> you are already in a white dress.—Olga, in *Three Sisters*

*O*ut of a brown-paper cocoon
let a pale dress be wrestled
into resurrection from winter's long wrap.
Blanched in buttermilk and lemon,

moth wing fed by laundress through mangle,
let the white dress dangle in the afterlife
clothes pegs lift from the earth below.
Let it fall from starch's grace

and bleach under the full-blown moon
that last year sharpened its scythe
until a final sliver cut into cloud
over the ghost of an orchard

where each blossom opened farther,
a powdery mouthful of water
quenching the petals that withered around it.
Let the hand-stitched lawn lie sprawled,

a last patch of that snow holding,
dear life, where sleep cleaves to shade.
Though ground warms enough to be broken again,
on this the youngest's name day

let her shrug off the year's crêpe.
In a dressing room somewhere backstage
shared with the blue, the black gowns
of the two cast as her sisters,

let an actress shed her own clothes
for the white dress, calling up the first
of the words put to her mouth in the play
of a life borrowed against another.

A SNAPSHOT

> Life will get the better of you.
> —Vershinin, in *Three Sisters*

The schoolmaster's forgotten the present
he already gave his sister-in-law:
here's his little history of the school,

another copy. She can't recall
how that window or this ceiling
would be spoken of in Italian;

and the song about an oak tree by the sea,
with a green *blank*, then *something* gold,
haunts his wife, who hums again the part she knows.

The doctor's noted down a cure
for baldness, then scratched it out.
Just before lunch they had their photograph taken,

a new leaf for the album to press
under its gathering dust.
Who is the one whose face lies in shadow?

THE WINGS

*F*rom battlement to keep,
the ice palace wept itself a moat.
No more would mummers skate away the chill,
their breath fog the ballroom's blue cave,

nor ice candles dipped in kerosene be set aflame.
A hand that coolly checked a brow for fever
would dissolve its imprint into those walls
of water held together by water. Downstream,

starched nurse navigating from bedside to bed,
the first floe charted toward reopened sea,
past an iceboat about to reverse engines homeward.
A warmed column of air filled with the cries

of heavy gray birds guiding one another higher
until the only cranes left in the province
stalked a folding Japanese screen
carved next to a bed with linens of ice

whose pillows melted, tear into tear.
Feet in a pond where before they'd waded
in icicles' stubble, the birds held, breathless,
the hush a taxidermist would labor to catch,

stretching a skin he's tanned
over gauze-dressed plaster, faded feathers dyed
to mimic the transient tinge of the living.
Then the glass eyes.

THE NEXT ACT

Between vistas painted into vastness
onstage and the cramped quarters off,
a young soldier girds for a last scene

before his brigade moves out,
the thirty-nine words assigned him to deliver
waiting final polish under his breath.

A shallow sigh mists an untarnished buckle
he buffs by rote with a heavy sleeve.
"Goodbye, echo." "Goodbye, trees."

THE AFTERLIFE OF THINGS

*I*nto the disguise of everyday
the actors pass, improbable

as angels and as invisible,
while here lies the mustache

that distinguished a baron
from a colonel, and his spirit gum.

Whalebones corset a wasp waist,
a pigeon breast of unrehearsed air.

One stained wing of a collar
flaps free of its limp shirt.

On the dressing-room floor
powder to gray the hair

has come to grief—O be the man
strolling without overcoat

a foreign city only an ocean away,
every dog and soap bearing the smell

of civilization, not home:
how distant the dead, just out of reach.

The earth turns dustier
than you would remember.

A Brief History of Blasphemy, for the Feast of the Assumption

Richland, Washington

What did you go into the wilderness to see,
a reed shaken with the wind?
In their white coveralls and shoes,
your fathers about their business?

Uranium bombarded until you must be cleared
to see it, the adoring *O's*
of domed reactors hugging the ground?
The prophet's airy promise of fir tree

roots in barren soil, thorns come up
in farmhouse, nettles and brambles in barn.
That much can be gleaned driving straight
through cheat grass and sage along broken white lines

painted past well-guarded emptiness.
Thirty miles from the new town
a graveyard shift labors, honey to be drawn
from rock, oil out of flint,

desert to blossom as a rose whose cloud
of petals billows from a stalk of steam.
Rising from the dead of August nights,
you switch a lamp to life and are blinded.

The clothes cast aside lie crumpled
until resurrected, this city no city of the plain
where a hive of workers swarmed toward paddy
or factory under a sky marked by a single plane,

its wings unreadable in the slanted glance of sun,
a plum-blossom parachute homing
to outstretched buildings the next instant
flattened into a pillar of smoke.

Fire and the local brimstone left to wreak
their lesser miracles, the fleet's dirge
to be sung in the valley, a choir to rehearse
some Christian hymns, let us celebrate

this newest holy day of obligation,
the Virgin's assumption into heaven
assuming her body, long missing
from some unremarked tomb, explained away

by doctors of the church winding her a shroud
out of their cleverness, shot through with threads
of regret at the untimely loss
of details as pure as her to whom they prayed.

In the Elephant Folio

Audubon's *The Birds of America*

A comb capsized on a glass-topped dresser
whose bird-edged mirror reflects
a round of lake—out the window,

water slicking back water,
an upturned comb of canoe parts huge wet feathers
until back into place they fall,

sleek as wings the anhinga holds open,
drying its subtropical laundry after a dive
into Plate CCCXVI. The painter hurried,

his kill of two dozen fading
like the opera capes of skin and feathers
laid out in the ornithological museum.

Pearls round the necks of the dead,
crumbling before bone to chalk.
The lake dragged for what

can be learned of the lost—it glosses
over kidskin slippers, tortoise-shell combs,
at no loss for weeds to wedge

between the moneyed bank and its own
murky business, host to more
than its mirror countenanced—

the blank side of a letter to a wife,
recounting two boxes of shells collected,
some curious seeds, 550 skins taken,

and 29 drawings complete.

Foolscap

Mote upon mote's endearments flung
after long-lost loves, gauntlets spoiling
too late for fights, petals and capes untrod

by untried brides: centuries of dust patch a tapestry
where moth-eaten knots have let go,
no longer holding their court of love to account

but counting out clouds swollen with coming weather.
One lopsidedly shapes the cap dropped by a fool
who mimed marriage—dowry's highly polished fork

taken by knife's sharp swipe. His bells are fading;
royal colors gray; snows have settled on a solid river
at one with skaters sluggish on sheep bones,

stroking upwind toward home and icebergs
of bread sopped in crystalline milk.
Frost's brocaded the window

a troubadour's half-frozen beneath,
lute untuning under snow-shot cloak,
curses to flower from his suspended breath.

In a stand of geese a scribe, unmoving,
waits a snowy quill's loosening, lambskin already scraped
and cured. Middle hours' devotions limned,

an illuminator stares into middle distance, unseeing,
through sunless noon, a spilled-milk sky
his palette can render only blue so deep-dyed

I look away—into afterimage, winter's overripe sun
sinking into blank page, dragging the day
with the wary wisdom of fool

who counts on nothing not cruelly kind.
Love's the undone. No, love the remains.

Snow White and Rose Red

*T*he bear at the door, begging
to be beaten free of his snowy coat,
was a king's son under a curse,
detail my sister and I learned long after

we scoured him with brooms and then lay down,
pale crescents pinned to his vast dark.
Rose claimed that in firelight
his fur glittered but I saw no more

than before, when a coin warmed in my hand
pressed a queen's profile into the ice
coiled in fronds against the window.
In the eye-size opening melted tear by cool tear,

had I seen something break from the forest's deep ranks?
I saw nothing beyond an animal knowing—
if it be knowing—what a lost hunter does:
on such a night any warmth will do.

So in the heart of a wood a man will sleep
inside the beast he's slain, waiting daybreak
to illumine the way toward any clearing.
Toward a cottage like the one where red roses

and white clambered to the window,
the sanguine and the snowflake's distant kin
spendthrift with promise of good company
as they vied for my sister's shears.

In a cut-glass vase too fine for the rough table
on which lay bread and books for two,
a bouquet would hold its salon
while as always we rudely, mutely read—

Rose, someone's travels bound in red morocco;
I, botany of the season ahead
where *naked* meant *without specialized scales*
and *tender*: *not enduring winter*,

the author looking out for those
after his own heart—*If it is too cold*
to read in the field, save this
for the warmth of home.

Shadows unroll across the bluing snow
but enough oblique light has pierced
a man-made pond gracing the palace grounds
that, out of a slow internal melting,

ice crystals regrow into bloom and thorn
as men harvest them, sawing the water
into frozen bales, loading sledges
tomorrow will drag to the icehouse.

The tree overlooking this—is it weeping?
Not markedly weeping.
Are the leaf scars solitary?
There are two or more at each node.

The bear, that long lost night?
He was one of two brothers.
One picked Rose to wed,
the one who had been animal chose me.

Wind rattles a fist of milkweed
until it's prized open, loosing a handful
of tufted halfpennies one by one,
that each be borne far off and root where it falls.

The Report of the Corrosion Committee

Mine to keep their minutes, which one motioned,
which seconded that they adjourn until
back from dry Khartoum their colleague steamed,
the foreign sun having shone as it had to
on his white legs before they disappeared
into grey wool, the Kilimanjaro
of his handkerchief laid flat before us,
tweezers lifting wafers of rust like hosts
for adoration to the perpetual
English twilight. Who would have thought
that I had anywhere to get to?
Teacups spread their atolls on reports
and I stayed calm, a tidy spot, anyhow,
off in a corner, nothing to be read
in sodden tea leaves I washed overboard.
I must have seen something amazing
besides the expensive delicate slip
I passed in a shop, walking duly along;
but for them it was not imported allure—
how well they understood the animal
imposition of filthy air
on impure skin, how it takes place while nothing
falls from the sky but rain's dilute solution,
sulfuric acid's caustic dictatorship
over empires broken up and sold for scrap.

About some things they were almost right,
my old masters. From the blow that would
draw blood, armor emerges unmoved;
but the humid kiss of atmosphere would waste
a solid shield to lace, electrons lost
surrendering to equilibrium.
Its portholes wide awake, the layered cakes
of chandeliers impassionately waiting
miraculous rebirth, an ocean liner
that did not specially want it to happen
skates a trench at the bottom of the sea.
The grand staircase devoured long ago,

the brass of railings guides the ocean worms
to a second sitting at the remains.
From its pierced side spills a river of rust.

And even as the minutes were read aloud,
something each owned was rusting. A camera beached
in driftwood's arms, shutter's one good eye
swollen shut. Blades of a pocketknife
refused to cleave kippers and cakes at tea,
or to scratch a blister of rust behind
protective coats of paint to estimate
its life opposing climates even worse
than this. Wet missionaries hard at work
even before they dried, converting harsh
remarks to motions rising from the floor,
those present in that meeting room then moved
that I record, by way of introduction,
how the committee on corrosion swept
as one through seas of charts and tables, change
of chairs, sweetly, like steel at sail on salt,
and how, rusting in other fields of service,
they'd never forget the time, etc.—
I to finish, I their memory.

The Diamond of Devotion

A GUIDE TO GODLINESS

*T*ransparent river pebble greasy in a boy's fist
before it's tossed, a toy, to his younger sister;

adamantine luster spied by a local official
who sold it for pittance to a peddler

who first scratched his name with it
in the councillor's window, then mailed the stone

to the government mineralogist who cabled back
every jeweler's file he owned had blunted;

crystalline carbon shipped to the colonial governor
who from state coffers paid the peddler mere hundredfold

and at the Paris Exhibition had its fraction of an ounce
venerated, relic of riches in the now's hereafter:

so gives out the vein now legend,
but let the stone sell again at the hands

of thief and smuggler, the cutter of brilliants
and the back-street one who recuts them into anonymity,

the broker god whose distant eye behind its loupe
magnifies the hardest of perfections,

to buy for the beloved proof of her worth,
soliciting for the lover the answer he desires.

THE SCHOOLE OF SKILL

the hardness test of Friedrich Mohs

After the talc the scrubbed miner dusts over himself,
    the green-to-gray of the dead, each Saturday,
but before the calcite clotting the hearts

    of each knight and lady undusted in marble effigy,
comes fingernail scratching in their names
    an empire from the mineral world,

demanding that any hardness softer
    than copper penny give.
Ever mistaken for other in the titled crystal family,

    often-flawed apatite
follows, minor intrusion into the igneous
    and the hydrothermal vein,

Greek for trickery, fraud, deceit;
    any gentleman's penknife would score
hatchmarks down its pallid or ruddy prisms

    with the blade that can't
incise into a window any more than reflection,
    gone, of a duel's scar.

Joints and the faults in bedding planes
    lay waste the mine's spoil tip,
kin torn from kin by the steel file

    tearing lustrous flakes of feld- from -spar.
Let the rasp roughen a perfect cleavage but leave
    unmarred the plane of weakness that

marries twinned quartz, one white mirror to another.
    Swilling ever finer grit, still
no lapidary's servant, the tumbler, rumbling eight weeks

over its semiprecious load, can match
oceans charged to abrade the facets, the fractures
    of the crystalline state,

polishing sand grain against grain till smoothed.
    Most abundant after oxygen, one
quarter of the colonized, cut-open earth's crust,

    able in number to segregate a beach,
rated 7 whether amethyst, agate,
    or arrowhead's flint,

starstone streaks a moonstone's half-caste,
    but bloodstone gives ground
to the tyranny of topaz, quartz capitulates

    as, next, topaz itself does, drowned
under the dust of sapphire's ungiving grind.
    What

volumes are cut loose, face by face,
    to release a jewel's ire,
what friction left to buff the colorless diamond

    into the dearest of love tokens
except itself—

A SWARME OF BEES

*I*nto exile each queen must carry her own gold,
the way a worker bee, burdened by pollen grains
bundled to her hind feet, drags the retreat
perfumed from flowered bed to hive.

Better a hem weighted lightly with diamonds
in the one coat allowed, better than coin
in my likeness, trading for bread.
Another chapter from *The Bluebird of Happiness*

left by someone in flight before me
fed to the fire, and the wall dripped honey
in beads lost from a dress I wore once.
No retainer left to do for me,

I scraped away the sticky sweetness,
letting it cement the heavy coronation ring
back on my thinner finger. Back of the wall
the mob of worker bees secreted waxen cells

that waited to be filled with food or young,
the uproar deadened through generations of wallpaper
into a genteel companion for roses' faded riot.
Besieged by no more than glacier's long march,

whitewashed hives buried themselves
beneath the warm blankness of snow.
In the half-sleep of half their lives,
her female escorts woke enough to warm the queen

by surrounding her. Stingless drones
she'd mate with, come the thaw, drowsed on,
even the one who, accident of genes,
would father a new slim virgin queen

who'd wrest the hive from her by right.
Before the danced-out language of the bees,
I spoke to ambassadors of kings blessed with sons
the common one of precious stones,

my loyal subjects those.

A PLANT OF PLEASURE

Out
of necessity
the vegetable plot,
but how to explain
the Persian for hunting ground,
paradiseoi, its trees planted in rows
so straight Spartan Lysander remarked it
as if that were paradise, become pleasure garden,
set like a necklace calculatedly flung from the terrace,
its dewy cut flashing sunstruck planes of cleavage at a wavering courtier.
Up the ladder of virtue he had climbed until, looking down,
he beheld the *parterre d'amour*, beds full of blooms bruising one another,
bees swarming a wreath for bronzed Cupid, greening the jealous air—
who would not plunge his cool mirror gleaming wickedly below
or the star laid out in carpet bedding, heartsease
past prime, boxwood holding the wild at bay?

Borage, happiness in love, has gone to seed.
Dandelion, old aphrodisiac, weed, has overcome
the formal garden, Mon Plaisir,
its sagging gates unlocked
shut, stuck letting
just anyone
in.

THE GROVE OF GRACES

after Botticelli

As wind blusters until blue,
courting obstacle with licks and shudders
and calling it love, setting orreries

of oranges spinning a heaven over the grove;
as cedars that ring the meadow
will split just ahead of the ax,

and the reasonable lily wait
neither to be trampled nor plucked
but to wear out its withering;

as the field mouse in its low weed-forest
labors beneath the owl's notice
where the oxeye daisy lets loose its petals,

auguring nothing of who loves whom,
the flaming poppy begging not to differ;
as two figures twine against a tree trunk,

wanting a room apart from this
as much as each other, passion sublimed
into bedlinens' two monograms made one;

as the painter in his best suit lingers
over gilt on the jewels at the throat of Pleasure,
then sheer drapery down the back

Chastity has turned to this world,
her veil glazed over flesh's marriage
of green earth and white lead

in a celebrated joining of lust and ash;
so the unstable diamond's pale hard fire
burning the mine's blue kimberlite

strains to be graphite's softer smudge,
its other half, snapped at the hand
of the white clerk who pays a black miner

a fraction of what they both know
a stone in the rough is worth.
On the paper between them, a speck

of the deepening dust raised by men
ordered to tunnel farther down,
who breathe it in: a decimal point

placed with the force of a period, so.

Ever After

*Y*oungest Brother, swan's wing
where one arm should be, yours the shirt
of nettles short a sleeve
and me with no time left to finish—
I didn't mend you all the way back into man
though I managed for your brothers;
they flit again from court to playing-courts
to courting while you station yourself,
wing folded from sight, avian eye
to the outside, no rebuke meant but love's.
Was it better then, the living on water,
the taking to air? I envied you.
When a king out hunting stumbled on me
in the nettle bed, I hid my blistered hands,
already promised to silence, to knitting us
back into family sting by sting.
Against his mime of marriage,
mine of no room for him was translated
as a tear-flooded dollhouse by our parents,
wept into his eddy of infatuation,
nothing left but for me to go to him,
bearing as trousseau the work cut out
into silence and your shirts.
I went gloved, and after dark, and lay by him,
still, hearing alongside his breath
something like wings far off.
So I told myself, and tried to recall my voice
as the nights shortened, warming to summer.
By day a pair of swans claimed the moat,
dipping and preening, the cob rolling
onto the pen's back, pinning her neck with his beak,
all too quickly over to drown her:
my fear the first time I saw it,

no martyr losing her footing down a bank,
just seamstress pricked by her own hand,
soothed by mud's dispassionate touch.
I suffered no unkindness—what then can I say to him
that I didn't more eloquently sign?
I envy you even the wing that maims you,
giving me, before you remember it,
a crippling half-hug. The swans' mute mating
until death, loss beaten to rage
strong enough to drag a sheep into water
and hold it under—how little
I've plumbed the nature of *happily*.

Princeton Series of Contemporary Poets

Returning Your Call, by Leonard Nathan
Sadness and Happiness, by Robert Pinsky
Burn Down the Icons, by Grace Schulman
Reservations, by James Richardson
The Double Witness, by Ben Belitt
Night Talk and Other Poems, by Richard Pevear
Listeners at the Breathing Place, by Gary Miranda
The Power to Change Geography, by Diana Ó Hehir
An Explanation of America, by Robert Pinsky
Signs and Wonders, by Carl Dennis
Walking Four Ways in the Wind, by John Allman
Hybrids of Plants and of Ghosts, by Jorie Graham
Movable Islands, by Debora Greger
Yellow Stars and Ice, by Susan Stewart
The Expectations of Light, by Pattiann Rogers
A Woman Under the Surface, by Alicia Ostriker
Visiting Rites, by Phyllis Janowitz
An Apology for Loving the Old Hymns, by Jordan Smith
Erosion, by Jorie Graham
Grace Period, by Gary Miranda
In the Absence of Horses, by Vicki Hearne
Whinny Moor Crossing, by Judith Moffett
The Late Wisconsin Spring, by John Koethe
A Drink at the Mirage, by Michael J. Rosen
Blessing, by Christopher Jane Corkery
The New World, by Frederick Turner
And, by Debora Greger
The Tradition, by A. F. Moritz
An Alternative to Speech, by David Lehman
Before Recollection, by Ann Lauterbach
Armenian Papers: Poems 1954-1984, by Harry Mathews
Selected Poems of Jay Wright, by Jay Wright
River Writing: An Eno Journal, by James Applewhite
The Way Down, by John Burt
Wall to Wall Speaks, by David Mus
Shores and Headlands, by Emily Grosholz
Pass It On, by Rachel Hadas
For Louis Pasteur, by Edgar Bowers
Poems, by Alvin Feinman
A Wandering Island, by Karl Kirchwey
Operation Memory, by David Lehman